RAF Scult

50 Years of Watching & Waiting

Edited by
Jim Baldwin

N Phillipson

© 1999 Jim Baldwin
Published by Jim Baldwin
Private and Commercial Publisher
Fakenham, Norfolk NR21 8LQ
In association with Fakenham Photosetting Ltd.

ISBN 0 948899 06 9

Dedicated to past and present members of
2534 (Fakenham) Squadron The Air Training Corps

Other Books:
Fakenham, Town on the Wensum
Another Look at Fakenham
Memories of Fakenham Lancaster
40 Years of RAF Sculthorpe
Hard Forms & Homework

Front Cover: *USAF personnel at RAF Sculthorpe with their*
British colleagues in 1986. (Below) Some 42 years earlier
the first members of the USAAF arrived and pose with
their RAF colleagues (Charles Sanders)

Back Cover: *THE Silver Pheasant under guard at RAF Sculthorpe.*
It was presented to the 47th BW in 1954 by the then Lord Lieutenant of Norfolk,
Sir Edmund Bacon. When the Wing left Sculthorpe it was placed in Norwich Library
where it was destroyed in a fire in 1994. A replacement was donated thanks to the
generosity of Sir Edmund's widow.
(Below) Lockheed C–130 Hercules are frequent visitors to Sculthorpe, those of
three nationalities feature in this photograph as well as a German Transall C160.

Origination by Fakenham Photosetting Ltd.
Printed by Page Bros (Norwich) Ltd and The Lanceni Press Ltd.
Bound by Dickens Print Trade Finishers.

A Product of Fakenham

From the Editor

Back in 1985, *40 Years of RAF Sculthorpe* was published, the airfield was a busy Standby Base administered by Det.1 of the 48th TFW at RAF Lakenheath together with the Ministry of Defence Police.

Today the living areas are private housing estates, the Technical Area has been sold off and the flying area is used by the British Army and the RAF.

There are many who were unable to get a copy of *40 Years* before it went out of print and at the same time more new/old information has come to hand making the story of RAF Sculthorpe even more fascinating. So the time has come for me to expand on my previous writings and produce this book.

I do not like to think of myself as the author of this story since much of it has come to me from colleagues and contacts who have done their own research and my thanks must go to them.

Brian Adams has been my 'plane spotting colleague for over 50 years. He, like me, goes weak at the knees at the very thought of a B–45 or KB–50 taking off from Sculthorpe. My colleagues in the Fakenham Local History Society have been a great source of information together with Huby Fairhead and his colleagues at the Norfolk & Suffolk Aviation Museum.

My late father in law, Sid Barber and, later, his son Derek worked the land that Sculthorpe is built on and so were able to give me the local 'feel' to the story.

There are many others who I must mention. Richard Jermy, Mike Bowyer, M J Milligen, Ian Crane, Malcolm Corum, Glenn Ludlow, Len Bartrum, Keith Mason, Murray Peden QC, John Laing & Sons Ltd, Charles Agar, Horace V Judge, Harvey Cocks, Don Brown, Bill Taylor, G E Watson Jr, Ann Wilson, The *Eastern Daily Press* and the Public Affairs Departments at RAF Lakenheath and RAF Mildenhall.

I no longer have who I once described as 'my men on the inside' because the airfield has now closed. So my thanks to Danny Goss, Bill Tawater, Gary Clements, Wade Marshall and Mike Varney. . . wherever you all are.

The wartime operations from RAF Sculthorpe are not within the scope of this book. However, the work of 2 Group RAF is well documented in books by Mike Bowyer and those of 100 Group by Martin Streetly. Details of the secret flights from RAF Sculthorpe in the early 1950s have been covered extensively in print and on television by Paul Lashmar and I must not overlook the work done by Peter Tearle on the Cold War deployments to the airfield.

Jim Baldwin

(Right)
RAF Sculthorpe in the late 1950s when the entire airfield had been secured. The 420th ARS can clearly be seen parked on one of the disused runways and the new munitions area is evident to the north east.

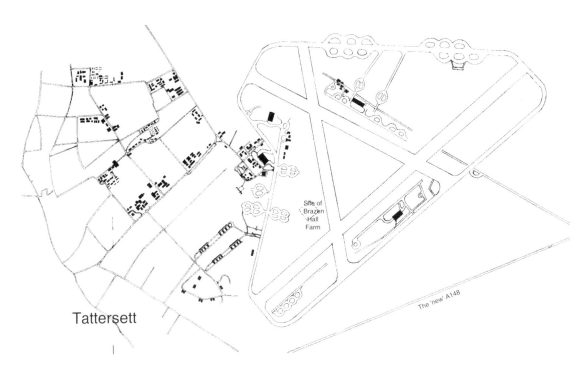

Site of
Brazen
Hall
Farm

The 'new' A148

Tattersett

A Sketch map of RAF Sculthorpe as it was in January 1946 when work on enlarging the aerodrome had stopped. Most of the domestic sites were still dispersed in fields and it would be another six years before all was fenced in. (Dave Stephenson)

An Aerodrome Is Built

RAF Tattersett

If you travel along the A148 from Sculthorpe towards King's Lynn in Norfolk you will find yourself on an unusually straight stretch of highway with road noise revealing the secret of concrete slabs under the asphalt surface. This is the diversion road built when RAF Sculthorpe was enlarged in 1944. Look to the right and you can see the airfield, look across to the left and you can just make out RAF West Raynham, the aerodrome which desperately needed a second satellite which became RAF Sculthorpe.

Work on this satellite, which is in the parish of Dunton but spilling over into Tattersett, Cranmer and Syderstone, was begun in the Spring of 1942. The work was initially undertaken by Constable Hart & Co. but some of it was entrusted to Bovis. They constructed the dispersal sites, the roads, the accommodation areas, the firing range and the Officers' Mess.

Bovis also undertook the building of the sewerage plant, although not without some trouble as the workers went on strike for more money while working on this particular project.

Some fifty men were employed by Bovis as well as six administrative staff including a site manager, time and materials clerk, resident surveyor and labour controller. The latter had a particularly difficult job as men were liable to be called up for military service. It became common practice to replace them with men from the Irish Republic, many of whom stayed in the area afterwards. Some of the workers were billeted as far away as King's Lynn and were brought in by bus every day, Newstead's Coaches of Syderstone being used for this.

Construction went on alongside agriculture, in fact, as the harvest of 1942 was in progress, chalk was being quarried from nearby Broomsthorpe and laid as runway foundations.

The aerodrome was literally carved out of the countryside, the only areas to be levelled were those required for the runway triangle, taxiways and building plots. Otherwise hedges, ditches and fields remained as they were providing they were not deemed to compromise safety. No perimeter fences or gates existed. Only blister hangars were supplied at first then, later a T2 hangar was built adjacent to the Fakenham to Syderstone road (this old road can still be seen running across what is now the middle of the airfield) while another was was constructed on the south side of the aerodrome in 1943. The aerodrome was given its own watch office (pattern 13726/41) which survived until 1948 when a new one (pattern 294/45) was built. Thereafter the original was apparently used as a salt store before being demolished.

Almost in the middle of the aerodrome was the farmhouse and buildings of Brazen Hall Farm. These were used as workshops by the contractors and then, later, the farmhouse was used by the Commanding Officer as his headquarters. The former occupants of these buildings moved to a neighbouring farm worked by the same tennant farmer who, incidentally, was saddened by the loss of some good wheat growing land as well as a farmstead.

Stange as it may seem, construction went on in sight of many German POWs who worked on local farms. One was heard to remark, looking at the goings on, 'The next war – Russia'. Did he realise that his predictions had a ring of truth about them I wonder?

When plans were being drawn up for the construction of West Raynham's second satellite one of the first considerations was what to call it! The powers that be approached the local GPO with the proposed address of RAF Tattersett, Sculthorpe, Fakenham, Norfolk, because the main gate was in that parish.

The immediate reaction of the GPO was that this was not at all acceptable! Tattersett was in the King's Lynn postal area while Sculthorpe was in the Fakenham area. Thus any letter bearing the name Tattersett would automatically be sent to King's Lynn and then be redirected.

It was towards then end of 1943, after RAF Sculthorpe became an independent RAF Station, that references to RAF Tattersett ceased.

The Squadrons Arrive

Although work was still going on, Free French airmen, together with some Polish airmen arrived at a bleak Sculthorpe during January 1943. They had come from the Middle East and had suffered the loss of two of their ships sunk on the way and were destined to form 342 *Lorraine* Squadron within the RAF's number 2 Group. On April 7th two flights of Douglas Boston IIIa (with a few Douglas Havoc Is for training) were formed under the leadership of Wg Cmd A C O Carver and Wg Cmd Henri de Rancout and the aircraft were given the code OA. 'A' Flight (*Metz*) was under the command of Capt Charbonneaux and 'B' Flight (*Nancy*) was under the command of Capt Ezzano. This all happened at West Raynham since the runways at Sculthorpe were not yet completed. It was May 15th before they were and 342 Squadron could move in. But there was drama on the first day.

A Boeing B–17 of the USAAF 8th AF 351st Bombardment Group, named *Fireball*, had been on a raid to Kiel and had spent part of the return journey trailing a crew member whose pararchute had caught on the aircraft when he had bailed out in panic. He was pulled in but was found to be dead on arrival at Sculthorpe. There was still some contractor's equipment parked on this particular runway so the B–17 had to run off it to avoid a collision. It was later pulled back by a D7 bulldozer. Another B–17, *Hell's Angel* landed with an engine out, two dead and three wounded and a hole in the port wing big enough to crawl through.

342 Squadron became operational on June 12th when it joined 107 Squadron on a sortie to Rouen. It was to take part in over 40 operations before moving to West Raynham's other satellite of Great Massingham on July 19th.

On July 20th and 21st, 487 Squadron (coded EG) RNZAF and 464 Squadron (coded SB) RAAF flying Lockheed Venturas took up residence on the aerodrome. These squadrons had come from Methwold and were to form part of the RAF's new 2nd Tactical Air Force. On August 21st each squadron received a de Haviland Mosquito FB6 and by the end of September each had a full compliment of the type plus a T3 and B4 'acquired' from West Raynham and never returned! Most of the Venturas were flown out, the rest remained picketed out awaiting disposal for many months. On September 9th, 21 Squadron (coded YH) moved in from RAF Oulton and it too converted to Mosquitos, the Sculthorpe Wing (140 Wing) was complete. Commanding Officer was Grp Capt Percy Pickard DSO, star of the wartime film *Target For Tonight*. He was later killed in action in 1944.

The first operation 487 and 464 squadrons undertook was on October 3rd, twenty four aircraft being despatched to bomb power stations in France. An abortive attempt to bomb a chemical plant in France was the first time 21 Squadron went into action and that was on November 10th.

All aircraft had bomb bay cameras fitted but these proved useless and so a camera 'plane joined the Wing and flew out on many sorties, many times bombed up himself. By now the aerodrome was very busy, almost 70 Mosquitos were stationed there and with all these aircraft around it was not surprising that dawn on October 23rd revealed two in a pile by the roadside! Luckily there were no fatalities although it seems that both aircraft were written off.

What happened was not in the best tradition of the RAF. A 464 Squadron Mosquito was returning home as darkness fell but had suffered a complete

7

electrical failure. Thinking that it was an intruder the watchtower switched off the 'flarepath' so the pilot aborted to go around again. The lights went on . . . and off again! This happened three times and by the fourth the true identity was realised.

However the pilot, Mike Sweeney, was now somewhat agitated, overshot the southern end of the runway and ended up by the far side of the King's Lynn road. A crane was brought in the next morning and began to remove the stricken Mosquito.

On that particular morning VIPs were visiting and the CO ordered two aircraft up to carry out demonstration low level bombing. Since it was foggy they were unable to drop their bombs and so returned. For some reason the first aircraft overshot on landing, ran off the north end of the runway, destroying the crane whilst the second did the same ending up like the icing on the cake. The CO's comments are not recorded!

There were other less spectacular incidents. A 21 Squadron aircraft had engine failure on take off and crashed, another landed with a bomb safe, but hung up, spreading his engines two hundred yards apart in the resulting heavy landing. There were only minor injuries in both cases.

It was not unusual for aircraft to return damaged and when one with a shot away rudder was refused landing permission the tower passed and instruction from the CO that it should climb to a certain height where the crew should bale out.

However the crew did not know that the CO was listening in and were continually muttering disagreements because the aircraft seemed to fly quite normally. Eventually they plucked up courage to bale out but at a much higher altitude.

At breakfast in the Mess the next morning the CO suddenly breezed in and made for the table where the recovered crew were eating and without stopping said. 'When I give a height to bale out I mean it' and walked out again.

These eventful months for the Mosquito squadrons were soon to come to and end. They were too far from the operational area of the 2nd TAF and so, on December 31st, the Wing moved to Hunsdon. In fact most of the aircraft of 487 and 21 squadrons were on an operation and returned to their new home afterwards.

464 Squadron had been split into two flights which had been on detachment at Ford and Bradwell Bay to learn night flying techniques since November.

The Sculthorpe squadrons had each flown over 100 sorties by the time they left.

From the Editor

Back in 1985, *40 Years of RAF Sculthorpe* was published, the airfield was a busy Standby Base administered by Det.1 of the 48th TFW at RAF Lakenheath together with the Ministry of Defence Police.

Today the living areas are private housing estates, the Technical Area has been sold off and the flying area is used by the British Army and the RAF.

There are many who were unable to get a copy of *40 Years* before it went out of print and at the same time more new/old information has come to hand making the story of RAF Sculthorpe even more fascinating. So the time has come for me to expand on my previous writings and produce this book.

I do not like to think of myself as the author of this story since much of it has come to me from colleagues and contacts who have done their own research and my thanks must go to them.

Brian Adams has been my 'plane spotting colleague for over 50 years. He, like me, goes weak at the knees at the very thought of a B–45 or KB–50 taking off from Sculthorpe. My colleagues in the Fakenham Local History Society have been a great source of information together with Huby Fairhead and his colleagues at the Norfolk & Suffolk Aviation Museum.

My late father in law, Sid Barber and, later, his son Derek worked the land that Sculthorpe is built on and so were able to give me the local 'feel' to the story.

There are many others who I must mention. Richard Jermy, Mike Bowyer, M J Milligen, Ian Crane, Malcolm Corum, Glenn Ludlow, Len Bartrum, Keith Mason, Murray Peden QC, John Laing & Sons Ltd, Charles Agar, Horace V Judge, Harvey Cocks, Don Brown, Bill Taylor, G E Watson Jr, Ann Wilson, The *Eastern Daily Press* and the Public Affairs Departments at RAF Lakenheath and RAF Mildenhall.

I no longer have who I once described as 'my men on the inside' because the airfield has now closed. So my thanks to Danny Goss, Bill Tawater, Gary Clements, Wade Marshall and Mike Varney. . . wherever you all are.

The wartime operations from RAF Sculthorpe are not within the scope of this book. However, the work of 2 Group RAF is well documented in books by Mike Bowyer and those of 100 Group by Martin Streetly. Details of the secret flights from RAF Sculthorpe in the early 1950s have been covered extensively in print and on television by Paul Lashmar and I must not overlook the work done by Peter Tearle on the Cold War deployments to the airfield.

Jim Baldwin

(Right)
RAF Sculthorpe in the late 1950s when the entire airfield had been secured. The 420th ARS can clearly be seen parked on one of the disused runways and the new munitions area is evident to the north east.

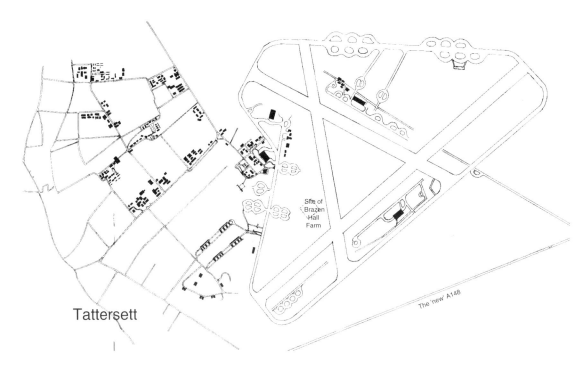

Site of
Brazen
Hall
Farm

Tattersett

The 'new' A148

A Sketch map of RAF Sculthorpe as it was in January 1946 when work on enlarging the aerodrome had stopped. Most of the domestic sites were still dispersed in fields and it would be another six years before all was fenced in. (Dave Stephenson)

Radio Countermeasures

On January 20th 1944 a number of Boeing B–17 Fortress's flew into Sculthorpe which was now under the control of 100 Group.

The RAF were not too keen on the B–17 since 90 Squadron's disasterous encounter with the earlier mark at West Raynham in 1941. However, the Americans were making good use of the improved 'F' model so the RAF decided to aquire a number, two Radio Countermeasures squadrons eventually being some of the recipients.

One of these was 214 Squadron, a real Commonwealth unit with personel from Canada, Australia, New Zealand, Rhodesia, England, Scotland, Wales and . . . Austria! Added to this the squadron had the suffix FMS denoting that the Federated States of Malaya had helped finance the purchase of some aircraft.

The squadron moved to Sculthorpe on January 17th and the first of its aircraft arrived on the 20th. One of these was an old Fortress I (the 'D' model) dubbed the White Ghost because it was still in its Coastal Command colours. This aircraft, AN520, had been in use since 1941 and it stayed with 214 Squadron until September 1944. The other Fortresses were F and G models which the RAF called Marks II and III. Some were secondhand USAAF 8th Air Force machines still in American Markings. These aircraft, 14 'F' models, were repainted, given the code BU and fitted out with temporary electronic equipment and then sent to Scottish Aviation at Prestwick for final fitting out. The others, 'G' models, went to Prestwick before delivery to Sculthorpe and some ended up painted almost black overall, including most of the window space.

On February 13th the first aircraft to go to the Bomber Development Unit at Newmarket was despatched and from then on crews went back and forth to carry out trials with the aircraft and equipment. As a result some modifications were carried out including the removal of the ball turret.

The RCM equipment fitted was second choice is seems, the original specification was for *Jostle 4* and *Airborne Grocer* but these were not available at the time so *ABC* jamming equipment was fitted. By the end of February 214 Squadron had 21 Fortresses on strength.

Attached to this unit was a small number of USAAF personel. On February 10th they were supplimented by nine crews from the 96th BG(H) from Snetterton Heath and were designated 803rd BS(Prov), the (Prov) being dropped on March 28th by which time they had six aircraft of their own and were under the command of Captain G E Paris.

The Americans instructed the RAF in the art of flying B–17s but unbeknown to the RAF they were learning about the British RCM equipment with the view to setting up their own squadron. This they had done by March 21st and their Aircraft, which had been fitted out with *Carpet* and *Mandrel* equipment, were then given the code R4 and were ready for their intergation into 100 Group. On April 25th Major C A Scott took over command of the 803rd BS leaving Captain Paris as the Operations Officer.

Four days prior to this, Wg Cmd D J McGlinn, the CO of 214 Squadron, led its first operation when a rail complex in France was attacked with the help of the squadron. The squadron was now able to offer five aircraft per night for operations for the rest of the month.

The Americans, however, did not become operational at Sculthorpe.

During this period, like many other aerodromes in East Anglia, Sculthorpe received a number of gliders. About 32, mostly Airspeed Horsas, were towed in by Armstrong Whitworth Albemarles and Whitleys during November 1943 and were under the charge of II Glider Maintenance Squadron. A certain amount of training was undertaken and personel from the other squadrons were often invited to take part, but there were no takers!

The gliders departed in April 1944 and some were later used on D Day and at the Arnhem and Rhine crossings.

RAF Sculthorpe was then closed, it was destined for something bigger, and by May 16th the RAF and USAAF squadrons had moved to Oulton, about 12 miles away.

The aerodrome had been choosen as one of those to be extended into a VHB base for possible use by Boeing B–29 Superfortresses should the assault on Normandy fail, or at least that it what was assumed.

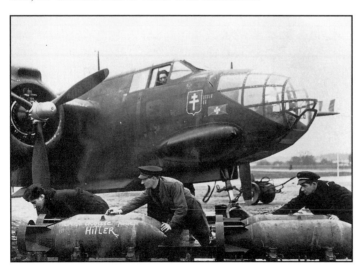

IF the nose art on this 342 Squadron Boston is genuine then the photograph was taken in early July 1943. Some of the airmen are still wearing their French uniforms. (via Liz Dilworth)

The Cold War

Preparations

As the Fortress squadrons were preparing to leave RAF Sculthorpe so John Laing & Son, contractors, began to move in and join the few Bovis personel who were working there. Laings had the contract to enlarge the aerodrome up to Very Heavy Bomber standard, tripling the runway widths to 300 feet and increasing the length of the main runway to give four miles in all. 7.5 miles of perimeter track together with dispersal stands also had to be constructed. 1,530,000 cubic yards of earth over 750 acres had to be moved and levelled and 566,300 cubic yards of concrete had to be mixed on site and laid, one runway requiring 11 feet of filling at one point. Many new techniques in runway construction were tried out and a laboratory was built on site to find the best mix of cement with local ballast and to monitor this throughout the contract.

The remaining blister hangars were replaced by two more T2 hangars to accommodate the expected aircraft. The extension carried the aerodrome across public roads closing the Fakenham to Syderstone and King's Lynn roads. A new road (known locally as the *Burma Road*) was constructed. Part of the old Syderstone road can still be seen going across the centre of the site. The other minor roads built over were not officially closed until 1962!

To help drainage two culverts, one in Sculthorpe and one in Dunton, were modified to take the surface water into the River Wensum, almost a mile away. The maintenance of these drains has always remained the responsibility of the military or their agents even though they are some distance from the aerodrome.

Some idea of the extent of the expansion can be gathered from some of the statistics involved. 1,400 men were employed, 800 living in the RAF quarters. 163 items of mechanical plant and 172 lorries were in use at one period giving 264 movements per hour on and off site. Special trains were shunted into a siding at one of Fakenham's stations on certain Sundays and up to 40 trucks cleared in a day.

Although the aerodrome was closed to flying for the duration of the contract there were accidents involving aircraft on the site.

On March 14th 1945 a Bristol Beaufighter (RD431) from the Pilot's Pool at Bircham Newton developed at fault and belly landed in an adjoining field when the pilot discovered Sculthorpe was full of buldozers! A few months later later a North American P–51 Mustang (unidentified) flew into the ground near the complex of huts that formed the contractor's administration area much to the consternation of the staff.

Work was stopped after 533 days, although many working days were lost due to inclement weather during the Winter of 1944/45, and the total tea consumption was then estimated at 2,000,000 cups!

An official description of Sculthorpe as at 1.12.44 lists accommodation for 1,773 RAF and 409 WAAFs. It also lists four T2 hangars and one B1. If it was planned the B1 was never built.

Since the war had ended it seemed that all the effort and the expense had been for nothing, but this was not so.

Crisis in Europe

In recent years it has emerged that the converting of certain aerodromes to VHB standard was not entirely the D Day insurance that everyone thought it was.

In January 1946 the USAAF and the RAF were unofficially having discussions about any possible conflict in Eastern Europe. Indeed, some special buildings 'for Air Ministry use' were completed at Sculthorpe and Lakenheath by the end of August that year with the special instruction that they were to remain untouched. It is presumed that these buildings were for the storage and construction of atomic bombs. It is also significant that aerodromes which had been upgraded to VHB standard were not used by the RAF but left on Care and Maintenance.

The speculation of 1946 was proved correct two years later when the Berlin crisis came to ahead. By the middle of 1948 the Americans felt that it would be necessary to have a show of force in Europe. This would be in the form of groups of SAC B–29s rotating on training missions in such a way that there would be three groups on deployment at any one time. It was not possible to station these on the continent except in Germany, but this was too close to the action and too provocative. The UK seemed the ideal answer. However, the USA was technically a foreign power in peacetime, having to get permission to even fly in UK airspace even though a 'Special Relationship' existed between the two countries.

Throughout the months of July and August 1948 the US made a number of unprecidented requests of the British Government. It asked for permission to place two (later three) SAC bomber groups, by rotation, in the UK with the RAF supplying ground support, munitions, food, transport and fuel. The British went through the motions of considering these requests and agreed to every one. Such was the urgency of the situation, and the British knew this, that the bombers were ready for the off as soon as permission had been granted. Such was the secrecy of this exercise that to begin with the matter was handled by the British Cabinet Committee on Germany where business could be kept 'under wraps'.

At this time consideration was also being given to making these arrangements permanent but agreement on this was not so easy to come by. It was 1950 before this matter was finally resolved and by this time NATO agreements were in place.

Aerodromes requested by the US for use by these groups were Marham, Lakenheath, Sculthorpe, Heathrow and Boscombe Down. The last two were not considered suitable and Sculthorpe had its usual problem of accommodation so the Americans were to use Scampton and Waddington until some barrack blocks and married quarters had been built there. However, these were not ready until the winter of 1948/49 so use had to made of the existing Nissen Huts which had not been use since 1944 except for those used by Laing's construction workers. They were in a pretty poor state, but then so were the RAF and the USAF, both having been run down rapidly after the war.

So, in far from ideal condition, RAF Sculthorpe emerged from Care and Maintenance in December 1948 and prepared itself for a wartime mission and following month road tankers began bringing in fuel. It was under the command of Grp Capt Parker with Sqd Ldr Eames handling the day to day running of the place. No doubt he was pleased to be in charge of the new VHB pattern Control Tower which had just been completed! *(Thanks to Peter Tearle for his research)*

TDY

The first American squadrons, the 325th, 326th and 327th Bombardment Squadrons /92nd Bombardment Group, arrived in February 1949 and commenced training on the 15th. They were the first of the many TDY units who were to stay for 30 or 90 days to train before returning to their home bases. Soon the airfield had its full complement of personel with around 440 RAF supporting 850 US airmen. However, because of the highly secret nature of the USAF mission, most of the RAF personel were confined to the Western end of the aerodrome. Those needing to work on the flightline or in the technical areas had to pass through barriers and checkpoints. In January, the USAF 7502nd Air Base Group were established to back up the flyers and the whole operation was on 24 hour alert.

There were many problems at Sculthorpe in these early days. Many of the wartime buildings needed attention or, at the very least, drying out which did little for the moral of the Americans although, one suspects that the RAF National Servicemen (of which there were many) concluded that this was their lot anyway!

Because both Air Forces had been drastically dismantled at the end of the war many of the necessary systems and supply lines required were not in place and those operating them were not yet fully proficient in the required skills. Even the aircrew needed to undergo intensive training. American supplies came in by road and rail, mostly from the new depot at Burtonwood in Lancashire and could take some days to reach Norfolk.

A lack of transport led to a delay in bringing in and storing munitions although there were visits by Fairchild C–119s which brought in some supplies and there are also reports that elderly Convair B–24 Liberators (probably the cargo version) called into Sculthorpe.

Some of the US/British agreements did not work in practice, noteably the eating arrangements. The US airmen would not reduced their standard to the rationed British and the RAF would certainly not raise their standards to those of the Americans! So the messing became one of the facilities to be duplicated. The old wartime problem of pay differences also raised its ugly head, the National Serviceman being on 12 shillings per week and the US airman on something like £90 per month!

In spite of these problem the two air forces worked well together. The USAF had to call on the RAF for many things until they could get themselves established. In return RAF Lincoln bomber crews were attatched to the American squadrons for B–29 training although the British Government denied that they were going to buy any (in fact they did in 1950). Whether the US flyers trained in the RAF Station Commander's personal Tiger Moth is not known.

The B–29s trained in flying, navigation and bombing, mostly on the ranges over Heligoland. At this time conventional weapons were used. However, in April/May of 1949 the 509th BG using Marham and Lakenheath is said to have carried out loading practice with a dummy atomic weapon at Sculthorpe although this cannot be confirmed. The 509th also had one live atomic weapon on charge. April saw the departure of Sculthorpe's first B–29 Group when the 92nd BG returned to the United States.

Then followed on May 15th the 343rd, 344th and 345th BS / 98th BW. One of these squadrons lost a B–29 (62141) when it crashed at West Walton while on a training mission on July 22nd. Two of the crew were detained in hospital the other eight were uninjured even though the aircraft crashed in flames.

These squadrons departed on August 15th and on the same day the 63rd BS / 43rd BG arrived staying until November 15th, receiving a visit from HM Queen Mary during September. The 63rd BS were the first squadron to deploy Boeing B–50As to the UK, in fact one of the aircraft was *Lucky Lady II*, the first aircraft to circumnavigate the globe being air-refuelled by a KB–29M tanker aircraft, a type also at Sculthorpe at this time.

The fuselage of *Lucky Lady II* still exists in the Planes of Fame Museum at Chino, California.

The next Americans arrived in November, the unit in question being the 23rd Strategic Recon. Squadron / 5th Strategic Recon. Group with their RB–29s. This squadron was replaced by the 49th BS / 2nd BG (flying B–50s) and the 2nd Air Refuelling Squadron on February 15th 1950, remaining until May 15th. Two days later they were joined by the 352nd and 353rd BS / 301st BG (flying B–29s). On the 27th the 72nd SRS / 5th SRG (flying RB–29s) arrived, leaving for Burtonwood in July to make way for the 340th, 341st and 342nd BS / 97th BW who were the first to use Boeing B–50Ds in the UK.

The 97th stayed until October 1950 and the 301st a left a month later bringing to an end Sculthorpe's role as a Strategic Air Command TDY base, it would be over a year before Tactical Air Command took control. At Christmas, the US personel who remained played Santa Claus to 135 children living in orphanages at Hunstanton (St Christopher's), Little Snoring and a home near Norwich.

Secret Flights

Having arrived in September, the USAF 7502nd Air Support Wing took over the airfield from the British on January 1st 1951, attached to it was the 7502nd Air Base Group with some Douglas C–47s and in February the 39th AAA Batallion of the US Army arrived to take over airfield defence, most of the RAF had left by then. The 7502nd ASW was replaced by the 3911st Air Base Group in May 1951 and it was during this month that the 322nd Squadron of the 91st SRG arrived, being the first unit to deploy jet aircraft to Sculthorpe in the form of North American RB–45 Tornados. Meanwhile Laings were still untertaking building work including the building of a Blast Wall which the Americans demolished overnight when they test ran the engines on one of their aircraft.

It had now become evident that the mission of the 91st SRG at Sculthorpe was to spy on the USSR. However, the Pentagon was reluctant to allow the USAF to undertake deep penetration missions for fear of provoking that country and was probably concerned about the safety of the aircrew if they should be shot down and captured.

The RAF were asked to help, probably because they were more 'acceptable' to the Russians and because the Air Ministry would allow this type of sortie.

RAF crews were selected and training began beside the Americans with four RB–45s were painted in RAF colours but retaining their American serials, they were never taken on the RAF inventory. The aircraft were kept in a closely guarded clutch near the centre of the airfield although they were often seen by the southern hangar. It was known as the *Special Duty Flight.*

By the Spring of 1952 all was ready and the first mission was flown in April. When it was completed the RAF crew returned to their former duties only to be recalled some while later for another mission which was then cancelled. Almost the same crew were together again a couple of years later for a second mission in April 1954. The USAF also flew a mission similar to the RAF's first one. The whole exercise is still, at the time of writing, shrouded in secrecy and both the British and the Americans consider it a very sensitive subject.

Talking in 1992 an ex 86th BS pilot related how, in 1955, about three B–45s were stripped of all identifying markings with the crews undergoing similar treatment. The aircraft went away for a day or two and were then restored to normality on their return. To this day where they went is a mystery. Later, sometime between 1955 and 1959 a detachment of an unknown unit based at Spangdahlem in West Germany operated Lockheed RB–69A Neptunes (only seven built 544037–4043) on SIGNIT missions to the Warsaw Pact borders, testing Soviet reaction.

Joining the 91st SRG on July 20th 1951 was a Detachment of the 9th Air Rescue Service of the Military Air Transport Command who flew Grumman SA–16A Albatrosses and Boeing SB–29s with large orange dinghies underbelly. This unit remained until November 12th 1953 when it moved to Prestwick as the 67th ARS having changed its identity on November 14th the previous year.

The Big Forty Seventh

In May 1952 the advance party of the 47th Bombardment Group (redesignated Wing on February 8th 1955) arrived at Sculthorpe under the command of ex-Dolittle raider Col David M Jones. It had been detailed to make it ready for permanent occupation by the Group and on the 13th of the month 14 B–45s of the 84th and 85th BS flew in although some were delayed in Iceland. At this time the American newspapers made great play of the fact that they were already out of production and obselescent. On June 5th the 49th Air Division set up shop – all part of President Truman's 60 wings promised to NATO.

The Group also had its support aircraft units which changed as its requirements changed. From August 1952 detachments of the 30th, 40th &41st TCS / 317th TCW gave the residents cargo facilities with rotating C–119Cs from Germany. C–119Cs of 10th,11th & 12th TCS / 60th TCW provided transport from October 1953, using the former's personel, until the end of 1954 when the Support Squadron of the 47th took over the duties. This unit remained until February 1958 when the C–119s and a couple of De Havilland L–20s left.

The 47th's Operations Squadron consisted of Douglas C–47s, Lockheed T–33As and the first Convair T–29A in the country. Later the T–33s were formed into the 47th Operational T–33 Squadron (some aircraft being attached to the B–45/B–66 Squadrons and receiving their markings) and in February 1958 these, the C–47s and T–29A became Sculthorpe Base Flight. Target Towing facilities were made available by the 7554th Tow Target Squadron who arrived on December 16th 1952.

The build up continued. By mid 1954 two other B–45 Tornado squadrons had been formed and took part in *Exercise Dividend*, a UK Air Defence exercise. The 422nd BS(L) was reactivated at Sculthorpe on January 1st 1953 and assigned to 4430th Air Base Wing. It went to TAC (405th FBW) on May 1st and then to the 3rd Air Force (attached to the 47th BW) on December 20th. It seems that this unit was redesignated 86th Squadron on March 23rd 1954. The 19th Tactical Recon. Squadron (Night Photo Jet) arrived on May 11th. It used RB–45Cs as well as a couple of T–33s and was attached to the 47th BW on arrival.

During 1955, three brigades of the British Army were tasked with training for a para-drop and securing an airfield. Under the command of Brigadier Peter Barclay they were to train in the west of England, do a drop in Germany and then at US airfields including RAF Sculthorpe. The problem was that the RAF had no aircraft available and so the USAF's 82nd Airborne was approached.

They had no navigators so it was put to them that the British would train the American navigators in return for the use of their Fairchild C–119 Packets.

The deal worked well and a drop at RAF Sculthorpe went well even though the ground safety officer's advice against it was not heeded. The Brigadier came to grief during the drop and gave an interview to the *Daily Mirror* while laying concussed. He had no recollection of the event whatever.

On June 24th 1954 the 7554th TT Squadron became the 5th TT squadron with its Douglas TB–26Bs and Stinson L–5s staying until April 1957. March 1955 saw the departure of the RB–45Cs and KB–29Ps of the 91st SRG (the RB–45s may have gone to the 19th TRS) and in September (20th) the 86th BS moved on detachment to Molesworth and then to Alconbury, a new base taken over by the Americans.

As its Headquarters, Sculthorpe was closely related to other 49th Air Division airfields as well as having a detachment at Elvington in Yorkshire where 50 men of Detachment II of the 47th Support Group were stationed for some years making it ready for use. However, although a considerable sum of money had been spent it was never used by the 47th BW and was closed!

These movements made room for the deployment of the 420th Air Refuelling Squadron from Alexandria, Lo, to Sculthorpe in October 1955. Their role was to refuel the fighters of the 20th TFW, also part of the 49th Air Division. Originally equipped with 10 KB–29Ps, it became the 47th's fourth squadron in November 1961. On its way to the UK the unit participated in operation *Fox–Plan*, refueling numerous F–84s en-route and setting a 24 hour endurance record by one aircraft in the process.

The US Army were still using Sculthorpe at this time with such units as the 172nd Smoke Generating Company and the 50th Radio Controlled Airplane Target Detachment, known as the 39th Auto Weapons Bat, who used the firing range at Stiffkey. They and their OQ–19D drones had been based at Langham since 12.10.51 and like the TT detachment they ended up at Sculthorpe. The US Army left the UK in 1957.

The 4,000 odd Americans based at RAF Sculthorpe made a considerable impact on the still austere Norfolk way of life, involving themselves in a manner of social activities locally. The locals had little, the Americans seemed to have everything!

They were not without their own on-camp entertainment however. This was of a very high standard with visits from such artists as Woody Herman and Jayne Mansfield and many local bands made their name playing at this and other bases.

The 47th BW was a large unit, too large for Sculthorpe, and it had several other operating locations. Elvington has already been mentioned, Alconbury, its satellite Bruntingthorpe and Molesworth were used to take Sculthorpe's overspill at one time or another. Langham was designated as an emergency landing ground while Little Snoring was used for storage. The old WWII Decoy Aerodrome for Bircham Newton at Coxford Heath, only a stone's throw from Sculthorpe, was used as a Radio Annex for a while and all construction work at Sculthorpe was administered from the 'Air Ministry' depot at Fakenham. Perhaps the most interesting site used by Sculthorpe was 'The Shooting Box', a building at North

Creake. This was some kind of communications set up of which little is known.

As one might expect the Americans rose the occasion when, on the night of January 31st 1953 the North Sea broke over the Norfolk coast devastating the entire area. The problem was a massive tidal surge which came down from the north. This, combined with a high tide, kept in by hurricane force winds which were so strong that some B–29s at Sculthorpe literally bounced around at their dispersals. Heavy trucks were tied to the wings to hold the aircraft steady.

Many service families were living at places such as Hunstanton and found themselves among the victims of the disaster. By the end of the first day cooks of the 39th AAA Battalion had served 1,400 meals and A/2c Reis Leming had made three sorties through the water at Hunstanton and rescued 27 people, for this he was awarded the George Medal. The same award went to S/Sgt F Kilpatrick and four other awards were given to members of the Wing. On Armed Forces day 1954 the Lord Lieutenant of Norfolk presented a Silver Pheasant to the Wing, a gift to which the people of Norfolk had subscribed to express their thanks.

When he returned to the UK in 1993 one of the places visited by Reis Leming for a remembrance service, was Hunstanton cliffs where there is a memorial to the 17 Americans who lost their lives during the emergency.

By now the local population had become familiar with the black smoke extruded by the B–45 Tornados and there was often excitement when the base received visits from giant Douglas C–124 Globemasters and Convair B–36 bombers. Added to this, since the base was also HQ of the 49th Air Division, there were often visits from the 20th and 81st TFWs who flew Republic F–84 Thunderstreaks from Bentwaters and Weathersfield. RAF Sculthorpe became an important part of NATO as well as being a welcome employer of nearly five hundred local civilians who were, perhaps, only a little surprised when, in December 1954, it was announced that Sculthorpe was an Atom Bomber base.

However, greater concern was shown four years later in October 1958 when M/Sgt Cunningham, a man with personal problems, shut himself in a 'special building' with a loaded pistol for two hours. The airfield went on full alert and a marksman was placed on the control tower with orders to shoot to kill. It turned out, however, that the bombs in the building were safe and could not have been detonated.

The matter was raised in the House of Commons some four years later (6.12.62) when the Prime Minister (Harold Macmillan) was asked why the incident was covered up and why the press were shown the wrong building. The reply was that the concern was that the man should not do anything foolish with the pistol and not that he might explode an Atomic Bomb, there being no 'fissionable material'

19

NEWSPAPERS helped the people back in Oz to keep in touch with 464 Squadron. ALTHOUGH the USAAF had plenty of Boeing B–17s the RAF did not. This photo shows a 214 Squadron aircraft over Norfolk. (Tom Butler via Murray Peden)

in the building. At the time the Americans took the incident seriously and one civilian worker reported being made to lay prone on the floor. During the same year there was another alert when an Atomic Bomb dangled three feet from the runway after a malfunction in the bomb bay of a landing aircraft.

On May 31st 1956 the 78th FBS / 81st FBW with their Republic F–84Fs moved to Sculthorpe, they were to stay until May 3rd the following year while runway repairs took place at Shepherd's Grove, their home base.

A Change of Aircraft

Throughout a cold February day in 1957 a number of Douglas B–66 Destroyers flew into Sculthorpe, a year later it was offically announced that they had arrived. The 19thTRS received the RB–66B and on January 18/19th 1958 the 84 BS received sixteen B–66Bs and by the end of the year the re–equipment of the wing was complete. Many of the crews were from the 34th BS / 17th BW who came from Eglin Florida to join the 84th BS.

The B–66 was a sophisticated aircraft but not without its troubles. In the evening of July 7th 1958 one ejected its crew over Walsingham and flew on to crash in the North Sea after developing a fault. It seems this was the third loss that month.

Since January 1957 the 420th ARS had been flying ten KB-50D tankers as well as the elderly KB–29Ps and these were in turn replaced by KB–50J types during February 1958 although a 'D' model was till in evidence at an Armed Forces Day opening in 1961, the KB–29Ps were then scrapped

These Open Days were in fact very successful, playing host to RAF aircraft as well as those from other USAF units. The first was held in 1954 and the last in 1961. Once again, on October 16–18th 1958, the Wing took part in a UK Air Defence exercise, working with the RAF. This one was named *Sunbeam*.

At the end of 1958 the recently vacated airfield at Langham was taken over as an emergency landing ground and it held that status until October 3rd 1961.

February 1959 saw the departure of the 19th TRS to Germany to be replaced in August by the returning 86th BS from the Alconbury, all three B–66 squadrons were together for the first time. Even more dependants were brought into Sculthorpe at this time and since accommodation was short a hotel in Cromer was taken over to house a number of families. In fact, at one time, only 100 American families lived on the Base – 900 lived off! The problem was partly solved when in 1956 the British Government began to build 210 'Tobacco' houses at Sculthorpe (out of a total of 1,500 nationwide) in return for £5,300,00 worth of tobacco.

By this time there were some 10,000 Americans living in Norfolk and it came as a great surprise when it was announced in 1960 that the Wing would be leaving during the next three years. However, there was no connection between this announcement and the fact that thieves broke into the base during Independence Day celebrations and tried to raid the safe where the wages were kept!

On November 3rd 1961 an aircraft dropped 3 wreaths into the North Sea in remembrance of the crew of a B–66 who were lost the previous week.

B–66 Destroyer 40499 of the 86th BS had taken off from Sculthorpe on October 26th crewed by Captains Brooks, Savage and Davenport and crashed into the North Sea some 40 miles off the Norfolk coast. Over 154 ships and aircraft searched in vain for the aircraft and any survivors and it was not until December that HMS *Shoulton* located some wreckage which was recovered during the next two months. On the wall of the Lifeboat house at Wells is a plaque presented to them by the USAF in recognition of their assistance during this unfortunate incident.

Closure Again

The 47th BW was deactivated on June 22nd 1962 and it left on the 30th. The T–33s and C–47s, which had become Base Flight in early 1958, left on the 22nd. The airfield was then taken over by the 7375th Support Group, with a couple of C–47s, as a weather and communications establishment although the 420th ARS remained there, and were joined by a detachment of WB–50Ds of the 28th Weather Recon. Squadron plus their own aero club flying two Aeroncas. In July 1963 Sculthorpe was taken under the wing of the 3rd Air Force. The first 15 civilian redundancies were announced during February 1964 and then between March 17th and 21st the 22 KB–50J tankers flew out three at a time and Sculthorpe was rapidly run down and handed back to the RAF on July 1st, the 7375th Support Group having disbanded on June 25th 1963.

With the possibility of the airfield being abandoned the local District Council put forward a plan to turn it into an industrial area although the County Council were undecided about the plan.

A MAN called at my house and said 'Here's a photograph of me in my airplane over Sculthorpe'!
A Fairchild C–119C Packet of the 40th TCS / 317 TCW being flown by Charles Valentine.
(Charles Valentine)

A PAIR of North American B–45A Tornados of the 85th BS / 47 BW over The Wash. (Malcolm Corum)
In these days of 'Cost Effectiveness' it is interesting to note that the 84th, 85th and 86th, Squadrons all operated a mixture of B and RB–45s.
Crews found, by accident, that the quickest way to load the bulky Mk5 Atom Bomb was to tip the aircraft on its tail!

(Below) BOEING KB–29Ps of the 420th ARS on dispersal.
Since one has a prop missing they may be awaiting scrapping. (Richard Jermy)

A DOUGLAS RB–66B of the 19th TRS stands on the ramp on Armed Forces day, May 1958. This unit worked closely with the 10th TRW which it joined shortly before leaving Sculthorpe in the Winter of 1959. (Richard Jermy)

*(**Left**) THE 420th ARS at work. Two Boeing KB–50Ds, one refuelling an F–100, an F–101 and a B–66. (Richard Jermy)*

*(**Above**) A BOEING KB–50D of the 420th ARS being inspected by the public on Armed Forces Day, probably in 1957 when it rained! (Richard Jermy)*
*(**Left**) ACCIDENTS do happen. A Boeing KB–50D of the 240th ARS breaks its back in a fire in July 1957. There were no casualties. Was it the same aircraft?*

Back in Business

The USAF Returns

The USAF, along with all other NATO forces were obliged to leave France in 1966. The 48th Tactical Fighter Wing relocated to RAF Lakenheath and Sculthorpe was returned to American control to support it.

On December 29th 1966 USAFE established the 7519th Combat Support Squadron, attaching it to the 48th TFW to run Sculthorpe on its behalf. For some reason, six days later, this order was rescinded and Operating Location A of 48th Air Police Squadron became the use for Sculthorpe, the occupants moving in on January 9th 1967 by which time the airfield had been designated a USAF storage annex. A further order was issued by USAFE on April 11th standing down the Air Police in favour of the 7519th CSS who were given two tasks. Firstly to operate Sculthorpe as an interim War Readiness Material storage base (for which 3381 tons had already arrived) and to support a drop tank and pylon repair activity. These activities were part of *Operation Freloc*, the USAF withdrawal from France.

Within 12 months Sculthorpe was given a more important role. It was designated a Standby Deployment Base and the 7519th CSS was given the job of restoring the now very derelict airfield to flying capability and with accommodation for the large number of personel expected to deploy there.

To assist in this task Detachment III of 1979th Communications Squadron moved in to restore the control tower and other communication facilities. Many of the derelict buildings and what remained of their fittings were sold off and the areas grassed over. By 1970 Sculthorpe had also become OLA 48th Tactical Hospital bringing the station complement to around 150 US airmen plus a number of civilians besides the contractors.

By March 31st 1971 all was completed, later that year and early in 1972 munitions were brought in for storage in the Munitions Storage Area. Negotiations were already underway concerning the use of RAF Sculthorpe for an exercise called *Flintlock V*, a combined US Army and USAF deployment exercise and, on September 3rd 1972, a Lockheed C–5 Galaxy landed at RAF Sculthorpe, the first aircraft to do so since the USAF had left eight years ealier.

Another *Flintlock* was held in 1973 and an even longer one in 1975. Thus the scene was set. For this was to be the type of activity at RAF Sculthorpe for the next fifteen years.

Following the end of the 1975 Flintlock exercise yet another task was assigned to Sculthorpe. The French Air Force were returning a number of aircraft purchased with funds from the US Offshore Procurement Program in the 1960s. These were mostly North American F–100 Super Sabres (although in April 1976 Mystére IVs started to arrive as well. Later still a number of T–33s were included, some from Belgium).

Under instructions from DPDO at RAF Molesworth the aircraft were demilitarised and either scrapped or loaned out.

On November 25th 1975 three French pilots landed their aircraft at RAF Sculthorpe. Thirty two years earlier their predecessors had been the first to use the airfield.

Work on restoring Sculthorpe was still going on and by September 1975 50 per cent of the derelict buildings had been cleared away and the ground landscaped over. A gale in February 1976 caused $11,000 worth of damage but in spite of this the exercise was completed by April of that year. Later, in July, the Aggressor Squadron from RAF Alconbury carried out Gas and Go operations with a turnaround and refueling time of 20 minutes. When they returned again in October the time had been improved to 12–15 minutes. The last visitors of the year were the British Territorial Army who held manouvres throughout December.

Repairs and Summer Visitors

The 7519th CSS was disbanded in the Springtime of 1976 and, following a new policy, the Standby Base was being handed over to the Ministry of Defence. Sculthorpe became Detachment 1 of the 48th TFW. Only six USAF personel were allocated to RAF Sculthorpe but in reality there were many more because this small number was not able to perform all the tasks required and airmen had to be borrowed until the required number of MoD posts had been filled. The shortage of manpower became acute in July and the USAF recognised this, sanctioning (it seems) the use of the extra men. By the end of the year most of the billets and social facilities used by the USAF residents at Sculthorpe had been shut down, the balance were to close early in 1977. At the same time the housing was being upgraded with the view to it being used by overflow families from the parent station of RAF Lakenheath and the small cadre of people from of the 48th TFW who were now running Sculthorpe with the MoD.

SOME wartime buildings still remain at RAF Sculthorpe. The Armoury (**Above**) was demolished in 1997 (Brian Adams) while the Bomber Trainer building (**Above right**) was demolished a year or two after this picture was taken in 1968.

(**Right**) A LOCKEED C–5A Galaxy lands at RAF Sculthorpe on September 3rd 1972, the first aircraft to use the airfield since 1964.

(**Bottom**) A FRENCH pilot returns his North American F–100 to the USAF on November 25th 1975.

In May 1977 a new shape appeared on the skyline of Sculthorpe airfield. Wimpey Asphalt Ltd had been awarded the contract to re-surface the main runway (06–24). They constructed a huge silo to mix the 35,000 tonnes of asphalt and 5000 tonnes of friction material needed for the 9,000 metre length. A new type of material was devised by the Property Services Agency which consisted of single size stones bound in butmen allowing the water to drain away and prevent aircraft from aquaplaning. The operation cost £1,000,000 and was completed by December 7th, at the same time the hangars were repainted.

By early 1978 the airfield had returned to its job of accepting ex French aircraft for disposal and in January T–33s were joining the F and TF–100s and Mystére IVs for cutting up or selling for scrap at £1,600 each. Many of the aircraft found their way to museums or gate pedestals and USAF appointed M/Sgt Mike Weirs as a liason officer in this operation. These aircraft were put on permanent loan for technical reasons.

The airfield was now ready for flying again and on March 24th the Americans began an exercise, *Flintlock 78*, with the 72nd Signals Brigade US Army using West Raynham.

The exercise ended on June 8th and was promptly followed by another when 17 Republic F–105D Thunderchiefs (plus twoTF105Fs) arrived a day late for exercise *Coronet Eagle*. These units were the 465th TFS / 507th TFG / 301st TFW, a reserve group from Tinker AFB Oaklahoma mobilised for this two week training stint in the UK. They were accompanied by their supporting ground staff of 250. The fighters were wearing the code SH on their tails and those who visited the base on their open day saw the Commander's aircraft with *East Anglian Express* painted on its nosewheel doors.

To compensate for the noise of these aircraft many local dignitaries were invited to a barbecue and the local Police Inspector was made an Honorary Deputy Sheriff by the Americans. The Thunderchiefs left on June 23rd and later that day two C–141s took away most of the support personnel.

A REPUBLIC F–105D of 456th Squadron of the 507th TFG / 301st TFW on arrival at Sculthorpe on 8th June 1978, ready for 'Coronet Eagle',

The RAF Return

Tankers and Target Towers

Because the USAF had used RAF Sculthorpe for so many years it was easy to forget that it was still and RAF Station and it was quite an occasion when the RAF returned there in July 1978 for the first time in 44 years. At lunchtime on the 4th, Victor K2 Tankers of 55 and 57 Squadrons from RAF Marham began to arrive for their temporary stay while contractors worked on their runway at their West Norfolk home.

As well as the 19 Victors, 100 Squadron with its collection of Canberras also took up residence. Four marks of this veteran aircraft were used. B2s for target facilities T4, E15 for ECM work and two high-mileage T19s for navigation training. 231 OCU also boasted a couple of Canberra B2Ts. 232 OCU, also on detachment used the Victors of 55 and 57 Squadrons.

The only remaining approach lights at Sculthorpe were at the NE end of the main runway and as the days got shorter approach lights were installed at the SW end to facilitate landing during the regular night flying.

Two minor incidents of note happened towards the end of 1978. The civilian workers went on strike in support of their collegues working at the Polaris bases and a juvenile was reprimanded by the police for shining a torch at a night flying Canberra! Meanwhile the Americans continued to scrap the old French aircraft.

On February 15th 1979 Norfolk awoke to find itself cut off by the worst snow since 1947. Sculthorpe airfield was likewise isolated and remained so for three days. Then a convoy headed by a snowplough made its way from Marham and flying resumed on the 20th. Although nearly all the roads in the area were open the airfield was so choked with snow that, thanks to some splendid air traffic control, landing and taking off was taking place in both directions on the runway, movement on the taxiways being restricted.

Very few French aircraft were now in evidence but one of each type had been tidily parked near the maintenance area by the Detachment Commander, but it was not long before two of them disappeared.

Since all hangar space was occupied by the Americans any maintenance had to be done in the open or at other airfields although 57 Squadron did have the use of one hangar which they adorned with their fin badge. Work could be done on the nose of an aircraft when it was pushed through the doors of this building.

On March 1st at 11.30am Wg Cmdr M J Milligan, the Detachment Commander, lifted Victor XL512 off the runway. At that moment it was discovered that the rudder was not functioning. Corrective action was not successful and so fuel was dumped and the aircraft went into an emergency landing circuit. A Canberra was mustered to fly behind the stricken tanker to give a running commentary on events until it landed safely.

The Americans returned for an exercise *Flintlock 79* on April 5th and from then on numerous C–141 and C–130 transports flew in, unloaded their cargos of soldiers and equipment and departed. Again the 72nd Signals Battalion was at West Raynham.

Sculthorpe's most active period for many years came to an end on the morning of May 25th when the RAF squadrons flew out to return to Marham although work on that station was not yet complete.

Early in the morning of November 9th a computer fault activated the NORAD early warning system which protected the area around Great Britain. During the six minutes that elapsed until the fault was rectified, USAF Squadrons in North America were scrambled. However, since Sculthorpe required 24 hours to activate it remained outwardly un-affected.

Exercise *Elderforest 80* was the only signifcant event on the 1980 calendar. It began officially on April 16th but the first aircraft were not logged until the 19th.

The 1981 exercise was named *Flintlock 81* which began around April 13th and this time there was a great deal of flying involving C–130s of various types, C–141s as well as UH–I Ns, C–12s and a Vertol CH–47 Chinook.

Some of the 1,000 Americans flown in to take part had overflowed to nearby West Raynham, and a taxi service using a Beech C–12 was sometimes used between the airfields. The exercise itself closed on May 23rd.

In the Spring of 1981 RAF Sculthorpe embarked on a project which the authorities choose to keep very tight-lipped about.

The Danish Airforce was flying in surplus North American F–100s and Lockheed F–104 Starfighters. While at Sculthorpe these were being painted in Turkish markings and then flown to Turkey by crews flown in by Transall C160 and Lockheed C–130 transports while some Danes were collected by C–47s. This continued until about the end of October with the fighters flying in two or three at a time, and while this was going on ex-French T–33s and Mystére IVs were still coming in for scrapping. Some Belgian and French T–33s also went to Turkey.

The anniversary of the dropping of the Atomic Bombs on Hiroshima and Nagasaki was marked by a local CND vigil on the grass verge near the airfield. Unfortunately the distraction apparently caused two motor accidents so the campaigners moved to complete their 80 hour vigil at another spot.

More RAF

The sight of nine Lockheed Hercules taking off in a stick is quite an impressive one. This unusual sight for Norfolk was witnessed by anyone who happened to be near Sculthorpe just after lunch on February 21st 1982. It was certainly a fine opening to yet another varied and busy year for the airfield.

The Hercules were part of a joint British Army and RAF exercise code named *Green Lanyard* Thirteen aircraft were deployed to Sculthorpe (*Farmer*) where the Army HQ was set up in a hangar near the King's Lynn road. From there some 300 troops from the 5th Infantry Brigade, the 2nd and 3rd Battalions of the Parachute Regiment, were flown to Watton (*Dentist*) and dropped on the disused airfield. Some were dropped at Totten Warren and others at Frog Hill, both on the Army's large training area in Breckland, there were nearly 1,000 paradrops in all.

The exercise lasted three days and was reported to have been a great success.

While *Flintlock 82* was in progress, from the beginning of April until the end of May, the airfield continued its job of disposing of French aircraft and two batches of three Mystéres arrived during this time.

It was now the turn of RAF Coltishall to have its runway resurfaced and, like Marham's squadrons, the Coltishall Jaguars were to use Sculthorpe on a temporary basis while the work was being done. On June 15th numbers 6, 41 and 54 Squadrons flew in while the Jaguar OCU went to Scotland and with C Flight of 202 Squadron remaining with its Sea King helicopters at its home base, after all, they did not need the runway! In addition to Coltishall's regular squadrons, visiting aircraft which would normally have gone there came to Sculthorpe instead, making it a paradise for aircraft spotters!

Problems manifested themselves during the repairs to the runway at the Jaguar's home base and on November 1st it was announced that the squadrons would be they would be staying for an extra month.

At last work on the Coltishall runways was completed and on December 17th the Jaguar squadrons flew home although some had flown back at weekends for maintenance, the contractors having been obliged to leave half the runway clear.

*ONE of 57 Squadron's Victor K2s landing at a very cold Sculthorpe in February 1979 (Brian Adams) **(Left)** while a Jaguar T2 of one of the Coltishall Squadrons makes a landing in the summer sunshine of June 1982 **(Below)**.*

VOUGHT A–7D Corsair IIs of the Air National Guard were regular visitors to RAF Sculthorpe. These, from the 121st Tactical Fighter Wing, are lined up for public viewing in June 1986.

Aardvark

The USAF Returns Again

The General Dynamics F–111 *Aardvark* was a remarkable aircraft for its day. It featured the British invented Swing Wing and, to quote USAF Colonel Edward R Bracken, it could '. . . go pretty damn fast man!' In addition, the F–111 was fitted with the Pave Tac system of targeting and weapons delivery giving it a strike accuracy of 95 per cent. Its firepower was equal to about 2,000 Second World War Lancaster bombers.

Col Bracken was one of those involved in developing Pave Tac and so was a natural choice of Commander when the 48th TFW at RAF Lakenheath re-equipped with this type of aircraft. It was also he who had overseen the Wing's temporary stay at Sculthorpe while repair work was being done to this Suffolk airfield in 1983.

More renovation work at Sculthorpe began in late Winter. Fences were repaired and, for the first time in 20 years, the airfield was secure. Grass was cleared from all the taxiways and land bordering them was reseeded. Derelict buildings were made good and one hangar was re-equipped and and returned to original task of aircraft maintenance. Even though work was being done to the taxiways and hardstands some were breaking up and were unsuitable for jet aircraft to use.

The first visitors of 1983 arrived on April 5th. They were 22 Vought Corsair A–7Ds and two A–7Ks of the 166th TFS/121st TFW Air National Guard from Rickenbaker. With them were 12 from the 162nd TFS/178th TFG from Springfield and 12 from the 112th TFS/180th TFG from Teledo, their various colour schemes suggesting that they were secondhand .

Having taken part in exercise *Mallet Blow* these part-time fliers departed on April 16th after a few days of intensive flying, diverting over Fakenham in V formation on the way.

The US Army then moved in for *Flintlock 83* which made use of West Raynham as well as Sculthorpe. This ended on May 23rd.

The 48th TFW's deployment began on June 6th with the first squadron flying in at lunchtime. At the same time the following day the remainder arrived.

The normal complement of F–111Fs assigned to the 48th TFW was 24 aircraft each to the 492nd, 493rd, & 494rd squadrons and 12 to the 495th squadron which was a training unit. 55 aircraft used Sculthorpe, others remaining under maintenance at Lakenheath. Crews and other personel numbering some 400 were bussed in every day from Lakenheath while some used the rather limited accommodation on the base.

Limited maintenance was undertaken in a hangar designated *48th TFW Summer Quarters of the Superstars* as well as some engine testing during daylight hours.

On the 'Foto Fete' afternoon on June 25th three aircraft were brought out for the public to view and on this hot and sunny afternoon hundreds turned out to see them although a technical hitch prevented any flying. One of the aircraft on show was Col Bracken's own with his and his crewman's name on the side and with all three of the 48th's squadron colours on the tail tip.

It was raining and very windy on September 3rd when the F–111s flew home. There had been few problems at Sculthorpe. One bird strike, an historic problem here, but little else. Col Bracken wrote to the local newspaper thanking the locals for putting up with the inconvenience (very little really when compared with the extra income and employment it had brought to the area) and then all was quiet. Col Bracken's name was then removed from the F–100 gate guardian at Sculthorpe.

Peace Camps and Fighters

1983 was the year of the Peace Camp at Sculthorpe. A large rally at Wells-next-the-Sea was sparked off by the deployment of the 48th TFW to Sculthorpe and representatives attempted to hand in bunches of flowers to the Base Commander but were prevented from doing so. On the 38th anniversary of the Hiroshima Atomic Bomb the third annual Peace Camp was set up and was visited by a leading member of the CND, Mgr Bruce Kent. As Armistice Day approached the peace lobby had increased its activities at Greenham Common where anti Cruise Missile camps had been established and where much UNpeaceful activity had ensued!

Peace Camps were by now set up at 100 US establishments in the UK and RAF Sculthorpe was one of them. The camp was set up on November 8th and 9th and at the end of each day flags were lowered and the Last Post was played. A point was made, the few personel on the base knew little of what was happening and the airfield stayed quiet preparing for the next year's activities.

A unit who were to become regular short term visitors over the next few years visited during January 1984 and then again in February. These were the Sikorsky HH–53 helicopters from the 67th ARS at Woodbridge who carried out Night

Vision exercises. It was their predecesors who had lodged there 34 years earlier!

But it was in April of 1984, amid some controversy over the sale of the Married Quarters houses, that flying began in earnest. *Flintlock 84* began on April 9th and ended on May 29th when the first aircraft from the 52nd TFW from Spangdahlem arrived, the Wing's three squadrons were to rotate between Sculthorpe and two continental bases while the runways at their home base were being repaired.

The wing was equipped with a mixture of McDonnell F–4Es and Gs spread fairly evenly throughout the 480th, 23rd and 81st squadrons. Patterns of flying were rather erratic, some days, for some reason there would be no flying at all and on others you could almost set your watch by them in the mornings.

A Photo Fete was never considered until, out of the blue, a weeks notice was given of one to be held on September 8th when about 300 people turned up including some CND people who made a nuisance of themselves and also made the front page of the *Eastern Daily Press*. In fact this, and the announcement that new ammunition bunkers were to be built at Sculthorpe rather overshadowed the 52nd's stay which ended on September 26th.

On May 18th the MoD announced that they had plans for 11 ammunition Igloos at Sculthorpe and the local CND group were quick to claim that they were for Cruise missiles, a claim quickly denied by the authorities.

The announcement during the first week in January 1985 that Sculthorpe's Bomb Dump was to be extended and modified gave an additional excuse for fence cutting by peace campaigners. However, our narrative is concerned with the activities of the Airfield and on April 9th a Rockwell T–39A did Radar callibration in readiness for *Flintlock 85,* the first C–130s and C–141s arriving on the 18th. This time the exercise involved some 800 troops, the overspill detaching to West Raynham as on previous years. It lasted until May 25th.

Some of RAF Sculthorpe's buildings were now receiving contractor's attention and extensive work was being done to a couple of the hangars. By August, after a period of speculation and some controversy, 100 of the Post War married quarters houses were ready for sale, becoming known as Blenheim Park.

It had been strongly rumoured that *Flintlock 86* was to be the biggest yet, with some 2,000 troops involved, and with a duration of four to five months. How false this turned out to be.

Sculthorpe's parent base RAF Lakenheath detatched a number of F–111s to bomb Libya on April 15th 1986 which put Sculthorpe on full security alert the next day and caused much controversy world wide. The British government were not happy about this but the operation seemed to have had its desired effect.

More Exercises

The first arrivals touched down for *Flintlock 86* on May 19th, a week late it seems, the aircraft being on standby in case they were 'needed somewhere else'. This time there were only 600 men of the 11th Special Forces involved and there was hardly any flying. *Flintlock 86*, such as it was, ended on May 31st.

Some old friends returned on June 7th in the form of the 121st TFW of the Air National Guard. The first formation of six Vought A–7Ds touched down at 6.30 pm accompanied by a Douglas KC–10A, thereafter the remaining three flights of six with their attendant tankers landed at 20 minute intervals, much to the delight of over 30 car loads of enthusiasts who had been waiting all day along with as many others who had given up and gone home.

The Commander of the first detachment of personel, Col Gordon Campbell, later explained that there had been only a couple of problems on the way over. One aircraft was not able to take off, a reserve aircraft was used an another reserve was used by a crew who had to turn back when they were unable to refuel.

This time the 121st were deploying the 162nd TFS, 112th TFS and 166th TFS, and soon 18 aircraft had been despatched further, to Germany it seems. After a fortnight Air National Guard Boeing KC–135s and civilian Douglas DC8s (the first ever seen in Norfolk) changed over crews, doing the same again after a further two weeks. The final crews flew the A–7s out on July 19th.

Although it was not public knowledge there were those who knew that RAF Sculthorpe was under review as far as the USAF was concerned. However, by July, witheld money was released again indicating that the base was to remain in use. In common with other US occupied airfields Sculthorpe received quite a number of large concrete squares. These were placed on end around certain buildings and could be used as temporary runway repairs if required.

There was quite a flurry of activity at Sculthorpe during the Autumn of 1986.

Exercise *Hammer 86/2* began on September 13th, with the first of some 250 troops being brought in, together with their equipment, in C–141s and ever increasing numbers of C–5s. This was the first ever 'Patriot' missile unit to be deployed into 'real world training'.

A ground to air missile system was set up whilst other equipment was conveyed to RAF Swanton Morley, together with five other sites, and on September 29th the first of the mock attacks were made on RAF Sculthorpe. These involved Fairchild A–10s from the 81st TFW from Bentwaters as well as many other NATO aircraft, all coming in fast and low. The same day C–130s of the 435th TAW arrived to start their *Channel Herc* exercise, this lasted until October 4th and involved as many military personnel as exercise *Hammer*, which ended on October 20th.

Because of the uncertainty about the future of Sculthorpe airfield all facility and airfield projects were put on hold for a year. When money was once again available it was used on airfield work such as repairs to taxiways and seal joints.

There was some confusion at Sculthorpe in the Spring of 1987. Both *Flintlock 87* and *Hammer* were required to start on April 4th. However, it seems that the airfield was unable to accept both exercises at the same time although it seems more likely that the USAF were unable to accommodate them together. So *Flintlock* won the toss.

The exercise followed the same pattern as other years. *Flintlock* ended on May 23rd and *Hammer* began the same day. However, much of this exercise was deployed elsewhere, although a large number of aircraft, predominantly General Dynamics F–16s, attacked the airfield on a couple of occasions. By the end of May C–5s and C–141s were working shuttles to take personel and equipment away and by June 6th *Hammer* had ended.

For some while the situation in the Gulf of Arabia had become very volatile and the situation errupted on September 22nd when the American Navy came across an Iranian boat laying mines and used force to stop its activities. At 5.30 in the morning RAF Sculthorpe, in common with other American establishments, was put on full alert.

There had been local speculation about a change in status of the airfield for some time and this speculation increased when building activity commenced. There was considerable attention given to the taxi-ways and hardstands and a new warehouse for Prepositioned Procurement Packages (PPP) was constructed, the first building to be errected at Sculthorpe for 25 years! This was to house war readiness materials (WRM).

Messrs Kier, civil contractors opened 1988 by opening up the ground by the Bomb Dump on January 25th. Much to the concern of the local CND, they had the contract to rebuild this part of the airfield, bringing it up to the requirements of the 1980s and adding twelve new igloos. It had changed little since it was built in the early 1950s.

Flintlock 88 began on April 4th, with 1,200 troops stationed here and at West Raynham, while Watton and the Stanford Battle Area were also used. April 12th proved to be a most interesting day when five C–141s dropped 200 paratroops onto Sculthorpe and then did a circuit and landed. *Flintlock 88* ended on May 15th but within a month the airfield was active again. While the runway at Mildenhall was being attended to its TDY C–130 deployments, who operated under the 313th

TAG, would operate from Sculthorpe, the first of six aircraft from the 317th TAW (*Bravo Squadron*) arriving on June 10th.

An Open Day was held at RAF Sculthorpe on July 3rd. It was only advertised locally, nevertheless a couple of thousand people turned out on this rather grey cool summer afternoon.

August 10th saw the 317th TAW move out and the 722nd TAS / 463rd TAW move in, although the changeover took about a week to become fully effective.

The normal deployment of these units was 65 days and around a dozen aircraft were involved although some were detached elsewhere. While at Sculthorpe the squadron undertook various duties involving transport and training, and watching these aircraft proved how versatile and agile they are, little wonder that they are still being built after some 40 years in service.

The 317th TAW returned on November 11th, to remain until December 16th. The next unit deployed back at Mildenhall.

More Spy 'Planes

A Lockheed TR–1 was seen to use Sculthorpe in April, and over the following months this became somewhat of a common occurance, fueling speculation that aircraft from RAF Alconbury would use the airfield at sometime in the future. Although there had been further speculation about a change of status for Sculthorpe this was again denied.

The Lockheed TR–1 is a most intriguing aircraft. It looks like a Powered Glider, yet its single engine gives it a record breaking rate of climb, then, on the edge of space it loiters while its sophisticated sensors pick up everything and anything, probably me lighting a match! In the UK the USAF deployed the type to RAF Alconbury in the hands of the 95th Recon. Squadron /17th RW. It was while this airfield was undergoing runway maintenance that the unit lodged at Sculthorpe between April 18th and November 17th.

On February 14th 1989, the first arrivals for exercise *Command Post* came to the airfield. Unlike the regular springtime *Flintlocks* this was a very small exercise and all had gone by March 10th.

The eleven TR–1A's and one TR–1B (of only two built) began arriving on April 18th, completing during the first week in May, together with 250 personel, and soon began their routine work, usually first thing in the mornings! They made a fine sight climbing out in the clear morning sky or perhaps doing touch and goes, always with their attendant souped-up cars which chased them on landing so that they could be caught before the wingtip touched the ground. The out-rider undercarriage is jettisoned on take off and the main wheels are retracted into the body of the aircraft.

Sculthorpe proved popular with the flyers of the 17th TRW, they were able to not only use the main runway but also runway 13/31 which had not been in use for perhaps 30 years. Being a very light aircraft the TR1 was susceptible to changes in wind direction so having this facility was useful.

The ground crews were, naturally, not to fond of Sculthorpe. Although all hangar space was at their disposal it still was not up to the standard of Alconbury.

Old friends returned on May 21st in the form of A–7s of the 162nd TFS / 178th TFG and 112th TFS / 180th TFG / 121st TFW Air National Guard. They deployed 25 A–7Ds (including spares) and one A–7K for exercise *Coronet Pine*.

As arranged, 18 continued from first fuel up to the UK. One cell deployed from Springfield, Ohio without problems, but those coming from Toledo were fogged in, delaying them for 24 hours. The first six, plus the supporting C–141, arrived just after tea on May 21st to an audience of probably 1,000 spotters, some of whom had waited for two days. The remainder of the aircraft came in the next day.

They then moved out to various locations, returning to Sculthorpe for the final week when they hosted visits from various local groups and then, at 10.00 am on June 19th the first six took off for home followed by the rest at 20 minute intervals. The Support C–5 and C–141 left later with the luggage.

An Air Tattoo was held on August 5th and the weather was perfect. The RAF sent a good static display, but it was unfortunate that the American Air Force was not so obliging, although you could get very close to the TR–1s and F–111s. The flying display consisted of anything flying by, which was called in to do a flyover, and pretty impressive some of it was with displays from C–141s, A–10s and Canadian CF18s to name but a few.

Some 2,000 people attended and were reluctant to leave when the event finished at 5.00 pm. Most just sat in the sun on the grass and watched some of the aircraft depart, it had been such a pleasant afternoon.

More Air National Guard arrived on July 15th in the form of 123rd CESS (Civil Engineering and Service Squadron) from Kentucky (codenamed *Prime Beef*). Unable to use Mildenhall they set about doing some useful work at Sculthorpe. The unit is a mobile civil engineering team trained to do airfield repairs, making use of locally available equipment and materials. They returned to being Bank Managers and Shop Assistants on July 29th.

Flintlock 89 began on the 26th of the following month and three days later there was a spectacular parachute drop when around 470 troopers jumped from five C–141s over the airfield. There was a near fatality when two troopers became entangled thirty feet from the ground but injuries, happily, were surprisingly light.

A second drop was in total blackout conditions, the aircraft showing infra-red lights and personel wearing night vision goggles. One trooper suffered a broken leg when he fell into the Ground Control Approach radar dish.

During this exercise the 3rd Ranger Battalion US Army set up barbed wire entanglements and machine gun posts around the airfield as well as conducting (some very hairy) airfield security exercises. *Flintlock 89* finished on September 9th and the following month there were again alarmist reports that the airfield was to be used as a base for aircraft carrying air-launched Cruise missiles. As before this was denied.

On Armistice Sunday 1989 the Americans joined in the parade and service around the War Memorial at Fakenham. In his short address to the silent crowd of servicemen and civilians in the Market Place the Rector, Alan Bell mentioned the events of the previous week when almost overnight, the Berlin Wall had begun to be dismantled. It seemed that, at last, it was the end of the Second World War and perhaps the Cold War . . . something that Sculthorpe had been built for forty six years earlier.

VISITORS to RAF Sculthorpe view a McDonnell F–4G Phantom of the 52nd Tactical Fighter Wing

Exodus

The Americans leave - again

In many respects 1990 was like 1960, with an announcement that the Americans were to leave Sculthorpe. On April 17th the local District Council approved plans for a new fuel storage facility (to be funded by NATO) and *Flintlock 90* began at the same time with a large influx of troops on the 20th of the month. The exercise ended on May 23rd.

During the exercise the airfield was subject to a number of mock attacks by aircraft and at 12.40 hours on May 2nd, three F–111s from the 48th TFW at Lakenheath carried out such an attack, and even seasoned aircraft spotters agreed that the flying was, at the very least, spectacular! One aircraft, from the 492nd TFS, suddenly extruded fire, climbed, disgorged its crew capsule and then crashed in a field at Binham. The capsule landed at Wighton, the crew being uninjured. Local people attended until the arrival of the emergency services who had been alerted by a witness with a CB radio. Five fire tenders and a medical crew arrived from Sculthorpe very rapidly, as did the civilian services. RAF West Raynham was put on Emergency Alert but only a fire tender was needed.

On June 17th, a special service was held at Binham Abbey (Church) attended by the pilot of the crashed aircraft (which had remained 'out of bounds' to the local public for a couple of weeks until it was finally taken away. Indeed, a public road had to be closed). The Chaplain from RAF Lakenheath, and other USAF and RAF personel joined the villagers in thanksgiving for a narrow escape from disaster. (In fact some structural damage was caused by the impact).

On July 13th exercise *Coronet Lariat* began with C–141s and a civil DC8 bringing in the personel. The next day twelve Fairchild A–10s of the ANG 176th TFS / 128th TFW arrived. Tight security surrounded the 330 incomers and six aircraft deployed to their Forward Operating Location in West Germany while those remaining conducted exercises with Jaguars from RAF Coltishall. Some of the aircraft were seen with altered markings – and since some were suspected of being UK based it seems that there was a possible change over of aircraft. Ten of the A–10s left early on the morning of July 28th with two flying out later.

Storm in the Desert

Exercise *Coronet Gun* began on August 2nd. The 75th TFS / 23rd TFW from England AFB deployed twelve A–10s. These aircraft displayed colourful sharks teeth markings and were known as the *Flying Tigers*. Of the 220 personnel deployed, 60 moved to their FOL in Germany. However, no sooner had they arrived, when Iraq invaded Kuwait and the US, together with almost every other country in the world, moved military units into Saudi Arabia. The American operation was code named *Desert Shield* and as the build up increased some of the 75th TFS were recalled to the USA, enforcing the withdrawal of *Coronet Gun* from its FOL in Germany. Although the official end of the exercise was August 29th, there was some doubt if what was left of it could leave. In fact the aircraft left on the 27th.

As well as pilot training the 75th undertook a chemical warfare exercise on August 9th and, on the other side of the coin, the crews repainted the Base Chapel.

RAF Sculthorpe had been built to wage War in Europe, it had been used to deter War in Europe and now that Eastern Europe was voting out Communism or modifying it, and the Soviet Union was more concerned with trying to feed itself, it seemed that the airfield, like many others, had done its job.

The BBC 6.00 pm TV News ran a late item on September 16th, saying that the Americans were to close 150 of their bases world wide. It seemed inevitable that one of these would be Sculthorpe and this was confirmed during the evening when this Scribe began to receive calls from the press and, the following day, the local TV.

The Americans would be gone from Sculthorpe within five years. The MoD would not say if there were any plans for the place after that.

With almost immediate effect, Lakenheath's budget was cut and they, in turn, cut Sculthorpe's. All plans for upgrading (which had involved a new control tower, fuel lines, munitions, igloos and hardend aircraft shelters, all NATO funded) were scrapped. Economies were made with lighting and heating on the flying field and grass cutting stopped (this was later modified to 'cutting as required'). This made Sculthorpe expensive for any units wishing to use it for exercises and even the local Archery Club from Fakenham found themselves the victims of price increases for the use of the airfield. It seemed likely that the only visitors that Sculthorpe would host from now on would be the US Navy Softball teams who used the base for their tournaments.

As the year ended it was announced that RAF West Raynham, the original parent airfield of Sculthorpe, had a doubtful future once the Gulf Crisis was over.

On the August 2nd 1990 Iraq invaded Kuwait and while the US and the UK built up forces in Saudi Arabia with the help of twenty other countries the United Nations debated the affair and gave Iraq until January 5th 1991 to pull out. In spite of much diplomacy from the USSR the invaders stood fast and so under the codename *Operation Granby* (UK) or the more popular *Desert Storm* (USA) Coalition aircraft bombed Baghdad on January 16th.

RAF Sculthorpe was put on full alert with a high state of security. MoD police were issued with pistols and thirteen USAF police were brought in from RAF Lakenheath, being augmented by personel from Sculthorpe.

Obstacles were placed across the entrance to the airfield and a 'sleeping policeman' was built across the gateway with a shallow trench dug on either side.

Parking by the HQ buildings was forbidden and entrance to this was effected by going via the MoD police office and waiting for an escort!

Some work (pipe laying) of an unspecified nature was underway and at the same time RAF Lakenheath was taking away some of Sculthorpe's equipment.

RAF Sculthorpe was earmarked for three tasks during *Desert Storm*. It was to support the medical operations of the 310th Contingency Hospital at RAF Nocton Hall (returning recovered wounded to their units and dealing with bodies), it would have been a receiving airfield for CASEVAC and was to support RAF Alconbury if need be. Luckily things went well for the Coalition and the airfield was never called on to help, although it was a close thing at times.

Desert Storm ended after one hundred days and RAF Sculthorpe returned to normal except that RAF Lakenheath did not return what it had borrowed!

Many of the units which had used RAF Sculthorpe over the years played a big part in the operations to free Kuwait, their training there had been worthwhile.

In June, the local member of Parliament said that West Raynham and Sculthorpe could be used by British Army units returning from Germany. At the same time it was rumoured that 2 Squadron RAF would deploy its Tornados to Sculthorpe and personel to West Raynham when it returned from Germany in December. Its designated base of Marham being too full to receive it until 617 squadron had moved North.

Eclipse Bravo – a mini *Flintlock* exercise involving a special services unit took place between October 15th and 28th. The original plan was to move troops out of Sculthorpe and para-drop them at Watton. In the event they went by road.

Resident were two UH60As of the 159th Medical Detachment from Wiesbaden, one of which landed by mistake in the playground of the Bignold School, Norwich – not far from the Norfolk and Norwich Hospital. This happened on October 20th and the following day the USAF announced they would leave Sculthorpe by December 31st 1992, another casualty of the ending of the Cold War.

By now, rumours of the RAF coming to Sculthorpe were rife. The RAF's 2 Squadron were deploying to Marham from Germany as part of the UK's *Option For Change* Defence Policy. The spare accommodation at both Sculthorpe and West Raynham (another victim of the policy) was taken over for the personel, to be used until Marham's 617 Squadron was able to move out and two other units disband. Since this was scheduled to take some time RAF personel would be stationed at RAF Sculthorpe into 1992, but, it seemed, no Tornados!

During December plans were being made for a new year visitation by members of the Fakenham Local History Society . . . to label items for their museum.

The Man With A Spanner

By May of 1992 many of Sculthorpe's buildings had been handed back to the MOD and a new user was being 'courted'.

July 4th was a Community Appreciation Day jointly organised with Ross Foods of Fakenham. A huge car boot sale cum charity event was devastated by rain and was eventually contracted into a hangar.

The next day there was a car rally, the weather was much improved and it was well attended. Welcoming the VIPs on July 4th, Base Commander Major Kimbrell and Deputy Commander Captain Martin were presented with paintings by the Mayor of Fakenham, Ian Scott, and the Chairman of North Norfolk District Council, Heather Barrow.

Major Kimbrell explained that the base was the second largest in area in the UK, being 12 acres smaller than RAF Lakenheath. The main runways were still in good condition but because other airfields had now had their runways extended it now dropped from number one to number five in the league table of long runways in the UK.

After the weekend was over the staff returned to the task of preparing more buildings for handing back to the MOD and to clearing the munitions area.

The morning of October 2nd 1992 was fine and bright as a small group of people gathered between the gatehouse and the PSA building at RAF Sculthorpe for the closing down ceremony. There were no dignitaries, just one or two officials together with the Detachment Commander Major Kimbrell USAF and RAF Commander Sqd Ldr Rawe. The rest of the party consisted of the civilian workers who were redundant that day plus one or two people who had been connected with the airfield in the past, such as Colonel Harris (USAF Rtd) who was once deputy

THE 95th RS / 17 RW owned one of only two Lockheed TR–1Bs built. This one is having its photograph taken at a Open Day at RAF Sculthorpe.

STRETCHING its wings in the afternoon sunshine, this General Dynamics F–111F was assigned to the 48th TFW at Sculthorpe in 1989 (Brian Adams).

Base Commander. The MOD police had gone off duty at midnight on October 1st and security was in the hands of a private company.

The Honor Guard from RAF Lakenheath (Sculthorpe's parent unit) failed to turn up, but one of their McDonnell Douglas F–15'§s did, bang on time at ten past nine. It flew over the small gathering as the Stars and Stripes together with the RAF Ensign were lowered to the strains of a lone bugler from the Air Training Corps at RAF West Raynham, W/O Bandmaster David Hollingsworth.

After the colours had been returned to their various officers parts of the ceremony were re-run at different angles for the benefit of the media while the rest repaired to the empty PSA building for coffee and cakes (all served on disposables because all equipment had been returned to RAF Lakenheath).

Once the media had finished there were the handshakes and goodbyes, then members of Fakenham Local History Society removed the station name board for the local museum and it was all over, the Americans had left RAF Sculthorpe for the second time. During the morning one member of the crowd, dressed in a boiler suit, had wandered around with a spanner in his hand, it was now his big moment. He turned off the water and locked the door. Finale.

•

What was to happen to RAF Sculthorpe now? The housing had already been handed over to RAF Marham who were likely to need it for four years. After 133 truck loads of bombs had been removed from the munitions area this too was earmarked for the same RAF station for possible training purposes. The MOD (Defence Land Agency) were to keep the flying field.

•

At the time of writing (1998) the Tobacco Houses at Sculthorpe have become a village called Wicken Green while the nearby Married Quarters form Blenheim Park and the former RAF Sculthorpe school has been renamed Blenheim Park School. The Technical Area, now called Tattersett Park, has seen a few changes of ownership but despite rumours of various uses, including an air freight depot backed by businessman Richard Branson, little has has yet happened. The flight line and runways are in the hands of the MOD and are used frequently by the British Army and the RAF.

Sculthorpe Deployments

RAF 2 GROUP
342 Squadron (Free French) RAF
May 1943–July 1943

RAF 2nd TACTICAL AIR FORCE
487 Squadron RNZAF
464 Squadron RAAF
July 1943–December 1943
21 Squadron RAF
September 1943–December 1943

RAF 100 GROUP
214 (FMS) Squadron RAF
January 1944–May 1944
803rd BS (Prov.) USAAF
February 1944–March 1944
803rd BS USAAF
March 1944–May 1944

USAF TEMPORARY DEPLOYMENTS
325/326/327th Squadrons / 92nd BG
February 1949–April 1949
343/344/345th Squadrons / 98th BW
May 1949–August 1949
63rd Squadron / 43rd BG
August 1949–November 1949
23rd Squadron / 5th SRG
November 1949–February 1950
49th Squadron / 2nd BW
February 1950–May 1950
7502nd Air Base Group
September 1950–May 1951
352/353rd Squadrons / 301st BG
May 1950–November 1950
72nd Squadron / 5th SRG
June 1950–July 1950
340/341/342nd Squadrons / 97th BW
July 1950–October 1950

USAF PERMANENT DEPLOYMENTS
322nd Squadron / 91st SRG
May 1951–March 1955(?)
9th Air Rescue Service
August 1951–October 1953
50th RCAT Detachment US Army
June 1951–June 1955(?)
7554 Tow Target Squadron
November 1952–June 1954
Became 5th TTS
June 1954–April 1957
84/85 Squadrons / 47th BG (later BW)
May 1952–June 1962
86th Squadron (formerly 422nd) / 47th BW
March 1954–September 1955
August 1959–June 1962
19th Tac. Recon. Squadron (Night Photo)
April 1954, to 66th TRW January 1957
to 10th TRW *March 1958 – February 1959*
78th Squadron / 81st FBW
May 1956–May 1957
39/40/41 Squadrons 317th TCW
August 1952–October 1953
10/11/12 Squadrons / 60th TCW
October 1953–December 1954
Became Support Squadron of 47th BW
and 47th T33 Operations Squadron
Disbanded January 1958
Became Base Flight
January 1958–June 1962
420th Air Refuelling Squadron
September 1955–November 1961
Assigned to 47th BW
November 1961–March 1964
28th Weather Reconnaissance Squadron
August 1962–December 1962
7375 Support Group
June 1962–March 1964

TEMPORARY DEPLOYMENTS

US AIR NATIONAL GUARD
465th Squadron 507th TFG / 301st TFW
June 1978

RAF STRIKE COMMAND
55/57 Squadrons, 230 OCU
100 Squadron, 231 OCU
July 1978–May 1979

6/41/54 Squadrons
May 1982–December 1982

US AIR NATIONAL GUARD
166/162 Squadrons / 178th TFG
April 1983

USAF
492/493/494/495 Squadrons / 48th TFW
June 1983–September 1983
480/23/81 Squadrons / 52nd TFW
June 1984–September 1984

37th Squadron/435th TAW
October 1985

US AIR NATIONAL GUARD
166/162 Squadrons /178th TFG
112th TFS/180th TFG   121st TFW
June 1986–July 1986

USAF
317th TAW
722nd Squadron / 313th TAG
By rotation June 1988–December 1988

95th Squadron / 17th RW
April 1989–November 1989

US AIR NATIONAL GUARD
162nd Squadron / 178th TFG,
112th Squadron / 180th TFG   121st TFW
May 1989–June 1989

176th Squadron / 128th TFW
75th Squadron / 23rd TFW
July and August 1990

The suffix to USAF unit numbers indicates its task, i.e. TFS = Tactical Fighter Squadron, TFG = Tactical Fighter Group and TFW = Tactical Fighter Wing.

TO the sound of a lone bugler the Stars and Stripes are lowered for the second time at RAF Sculthorpe during the closing ceremony on October 9th 1992. This fine, sunny morning saw the end of yet another chapter in the history of this Norfolk airfield.